EMMANUEL JOSEPH

Rekindling Love: A Guide to Rebuilding Your Relationship After Divorce

Contents

1

Chapter 1: The Anatomy of Divorce: Understanding the Breakdown

Divorce is a complex and emotionally charged process that can leave deep scars on the hearts and minds of those who experience it. In this first chapter, we embark on a journey to explore the intricacies of divorce, shedding light on the fundamental reasons behind the breakdown of a marriage. By understanding the roots of divorce, we can better prepare ourselves for the challenging path of rebuilding a loving relationship after separation.

The Emotional Turbulence

Divorce is not merely a legal dissolution of a partnership; it is the unraveling of a once-intimate connection between two individuals. Emotions run high during this period, ranging from anger and sadness to confusion and resentment. It's crucial to recognize that these emotions are entirely normal responses to the upheaval of divorce. It's essential to give yourself permission to grieve and process these feelings as you begin your journey toward rekindling love.

Communication Breakdown

One of the most common precursors to divorce is a breakdown in communication. Over time, couples may find themselves talking at each other instead of with each other. Misunderstandings and miscommunications can fester, creating a rift that may seem insurmountable. Recognizing the role of communication in the divorce process is the first step in addressing this issue and building a foundation for improved interaction in the future.

Unmet Expectations

Often, the dissolution of a marriage is the result of unmet expectations. Couples enter into marriage with dreams, hopes, and visions of a shared future. When these expectations go unfulfilled, feelings of disappointment and disillusionment can creep in. Understanding the importance of aligning expectations and learning how to adapt when they change is key to preventing future disappointments.

Drifting Apart

Couples can also drift apart over time due to various life pressures and responsibilities. The demands of work, raising children, and managing a household can leave little room for nurturing the romantic connection that once brought them together. Recognizing this drift and its root causes is crucial for rekindling the love that initially united the couple.

The Role of External Stressors

Divorce is not always solely the result of problems within the marriage itself. External stressors, such as financial difficulties, health issues, or family conflicts, can contribute to the breakdown of a relationship. Identifying these external factors and addressing them is a significant part of understanding the divorce process and how it affected the marriage.

A Journey of Self-Discovery

As we delve into the anatomy of divorce, it's important to remember that this process is not about assigning blame but rather about gaining insight. It's an opportunity for personal growth and self-discovery, a chance to learn from past experiences and lay the foundation for a healthier, more fulfilling future. This chapter is the starting point for your transformation, helping you navigate the emotional and psychological aspects of divorce with the aim of rebuilding love, both for yourself and in your relationships.

In the following chapters, we will explore strategies and techniques to address the challenges that divorce brings, paving the way for a renewed connection with your ex-partner and the possibility of rekindling the love that once bound you together. Remember, understanding the anatomy of divorce is just the beginning of your journey toward a brighter, more loving future.

2

Chapter 2: The Emotional Rollercoaster: Coping with Post-Divorce Feelings

Divorce triggers a whirlwind of emotions that can be overwhelming and, at times, paralyzing. In this chapter, we'll delve deep into the emotional rollercoaster that individuals experience after a divorce. By understanding and learning to cope with these feelings, you'll be better equipped to move forward on the path to rekindling love.

Grief and Loss

The end of a marriage is akin to a bereavement, and the grieving process that follows is entirely natural. Feelings of sadness, anger, denial, and bargaining are all part of this journey. It's important to give yourself permission to grieve and mourn the loss of your relationship. Acknowledging your feelings and allowing yourself to grieve is a crucial step toward healing.

Self-Blame and Guilt

It's common for individuals going through a divorce to harbor self-doubt and guilt. They may question their own actions or inactions that may have contributed to the divorce. It's vital to remember that it takes two people to create and maintain a relationship, and placing all the blame on yourself is neither fair nor productive. Understanding your role in the breakdown of the marriage is important, but self-forgiveness is equally crucial.

Anxiety and Uncertainty

The period following a divorce is often marked by a sense of anxiety and uncertainty about the future. This apprehension can be related to financial concerns, questions about co-parenting, or fear of being alone. It's important to address these concerns proactively, seek support, and develop a plan to regain a sense of stability and control.

Loneliness and Isolation

Divorce can lead to feelings of profound loneliness and isolation. Many individuals find themselves separated from their former social circles or experience a loss of connection with mutual friends. It's essential to reach out to friends and family for support during this time and to seek new social connections to combat the loneliness that often accompanies divorce.

Rebuilding Self-Esteem

The emotional turmoil of divorce can have a detrimental impact on one's self-esteem and self-worth. It's vital to work on rebuilding your self-esteem and self-confidence. Self-care, positive self-talk, and personal growth can all contribute to a healthier self-image.

Seeking Professional Help

Sometimes, the emotional challenges following a divorce are too overwhelming to face alone. Seeking the help of a therapist or counselor can be an essential part of the healing process. Professional guidance can provide you with the tools to navigate your emotions and develop coping strategies.

Healing in Your Own Time

One of the most important lessons to remember is that healing is a personal journey, and there is no fixed timetable. It's perfectly okay to take your time and process your emotions at your own pace. Rushing the healing process can lead to unresolved emotional issues that may affect your future relationships.

Resilience and Growth

Despite the emotional challenges that come with divorce, many individuals emerge from the experience with a newfound sense of resilience and personal growth. This chapter aims to help you understand that you have the strength to overcome this difficult period in your life and emerge from it as a stronger, wiser, and more self-aware individual.

In the chapters that follow, we will explore strategies for managing and coping with these emotions, as well as steps to regain a sense of self and balance in your life. Remember, it's natural to experience this emotional rollercoaster, but it's also possible to come through it and build a brighter future.

3

Chapter 3: Rediscovering Self: A Journey of Personal Growth

Divorce is not just the end of a marriage; it's also an opportunity for a fresh start and personal growth. In this chapter, we explore the transformative journey of rediscovering yourself and rebuilding your life after divorce. By embracing this journey, you'll be better equipped to rekindle love, not only with your ex-partner but also with yourself.

Self-Reflection and Acceptance

After divorce, it's essential to take time for self-reflection. Understand that the process of self-discovery may lead you to confront aspects of yourself that you've long ignored. Embrace these moments of self-awareness, and strive for self-acceptance. This is the first step towards building a more confident and self-assured you.

Setting New Goals

Divorce often marks a significant life transition, and it's an ideal time to set new personal and professional goals. Setting objectives gives you a sense of purpose and direction, helping you rebuild your life with intention.

Nurturing Interests and Passions

Reconnect with activities and hobbies you may have set aside during your marriage. Engaging in your interests and passions can be incredibly fulfilling and help you rediscover the things that truly bring you joy.

Self-Care and Well-Being

Taking care of your physical and emotional well-being is crucial. This includes exercise, a healthy diet, and seeking relaxation and stress-reduction techniques. Remember that your overall well-being directly impacts your ability to cope with the emotional challenges of divorce.

Expanding Social Connections

Building a support network is vital during this time. Reconnect with old friends and make an effort to meet new people. Expanding your social connections can provide emotional support and open new doors for personal growth.

Learning to Be Independent

Many individuals become accustomed to relying on their spouse for certain aspects of life. Post-divorce, it's essential to learn to be self-sufficient, both emotionally and practically. Independence can boost your self-esteem and make you feel more empowered.

Forgiveness and Letting Go

Forgiving your ex-partner and yourself is a crucial part of the personal growth journey. Letting go of resentment and grudges will free you from the emotional weight of the past, allowing you to move forward with a lighter heart.

Cultivating Emotional Resilience

Emotional resilience is your ability to bounce back from adversity. Cultivating emotional resilience will not only help you cope with the challenges of divorce but also make you more adaptable and capable of facing future relationship and life challenges.

Embracing the Single Life

Being single doesn't mean being alone or lonely. Embrace the single life as an opportunity to focus on your personal growth and enjoy your own company. Self-sufficiency and contentment with being alone are qualities that can benefit your future relationships.

Setting Boundaries

Establishing healthy boundaries with your ex-partner and others is a vital aspect of personal growth. Boundaries help you maintain your emotional well-being and create a stable environment for yourself and those around you.

Creating a Vision for the Future

Ultimately, the journey of personal growth leads to the creation of a vision for your future. What kind of life do you want to lead, both in and out of a relationship? This vision will guide your actions as you work to rekindle love in your life.

The journey of personal growth is a profound and transformative one, and it's a necessary step toward rekindling love, not only in your relationship but also within yourself. In the chapters to come, we will explore how this personal growth can be leveraged to rebuild and strengthen your connections with others. Remember, your past does not define your future, and you have the power to shape the life you desire.

4

Chapter 4: Co-Parenting with Grace: Navigating the Challenges

Divorce often comes with the added complexity of co-parenting, especially if there are children involved. In this chapter, we'll explore the intricacies of co-parenting and provide guidance on how to navigate the challenges with grace and sensitivity. Successfully co-parenting can be a significant step in rebuilding love, both within your family and in your personal life.

Putting the Children First

The most important aspect of co-parenting is prioritizing the well-being of your children. Remember that they are the innocent parties in the divorce and should not be used as pawns in any conflicts. Co-parenting with grace begins with keeping their best interests at the forefront of your decisions.

Open and Effective Communication

Effective communication between co-parents is essential. This means discussing important matters related to your children openly and respectfully. Maintaining a cordial and business-like tone in your interactions can reduce tension and make co-parenting more manageable.

Consistency and Routine

Children benefit from consistency and routine. Co-parents should work together to establish and maintain a structured schedule that ensures the children have a stable environment in both households. Consistency provides a sense of security and predictability for the children.

Flexibility and Compromise

Flexibility is a key aspect of co-parenting. Both parties may have to make compromises to accommodate changing schedules or unexpected circumstances. Being willing to adapt and work together will benefit both the children and your relationship with your ex-partner.

Respecting Each Other's Roles

Respect for each other's roles as parents is crucial. Each parent brings unique qualities and strengths to their children's lives. Acknowledging and appreciating these differences can make co-parenting more harmonious.

Resolving Conflicts Amicably

Conflicts are inevitable in co-parenting. When disagreements arise, it's important to address them amicably. Avoid involving the children in your disputes, and consider mediation or counseling if you're unable to reach a resolution on your own.

Maintaining Boundaries

Setting boundaries is essential. While co-parenting may require ongoing contact with your ex-partner, it's important to define your personal boundaries to protect your emotional well-being. Clear boundaries can prevent conflicts and misunderstandings.

Moving On While Co-Parenting

It's possible to move on with your personal life while co-parenting effectively. Introducing new partners to the family should be approached with caution, and ensuring that your children are comfortable with the changes is paramount.

Being a Unified Front

Even though you are no longer together, presenting a unified front as parents can provide stability for your children. Consistency in rules and expectations in both households can help reduce confusion for the children.

Seeking Professional Guidance

In some cases, co-parenting may be particularly challenging due to high levels of conflict. In such instances, seeking the help of a family therapist or counselor can be incredibly beneficial for both the parents and children.

Co-parenting is a significant aspect of rebuilding love after divorce, as it allows you to maintain a positive and supportive environment for your children. In the chapters to come, we will explore how co-parenting with grace can contribute to the potential rekindling of love in your own life and relationships. Remember that, despite the challenges, co-parenting can be a fulfilling and growth-oriented experience for everyone involved.

5

Chapter 5: Reconnecting with Your Ex: Finding Common Ground

After the storm of divorce, finding a way to reconnect with your ex-partner is a pivotal step in the journey of rekindling love. In this chapter, we'll explore the process of re-establishing a connection with your former spouse, seeking common ground, and laying the foundation for a renewed relationship.

Reflection and Self-Preparation

Before attempting to reconnect with your ex, take time to reflect on your own growth and healing. Ensure that you've dealt with the emotional baggage of the divorce, have a clear understanding of your own needs, and are prepared to approach the reconnection with a positive and open mindset.

Setting Clear Intentions

Determine your intentions for reconnecting with your ex-partner. Are you looking to rebuild a romantic relationship, create a more amicable co-parenting dynamic, or simply establish a friendship? Having clarity on your goals will guide your approach and expectations.

Communication is Key

Open, honest, and empathetic communication is the cornerstone of reconnection. Reach out to your ex-partner and express your desire to talk and understand their perspective. Make an effort to actively listen and validate their feelings and experiences.

Finding Common Ground

Identify shared interests, goals, or values that can serve as common ground. These shared elements can be the basis for rebuilding your connection. Whether it's your children, mutual hobbies, or common life goals, finding these touchpoints can help bridge the gap.

Mutual Respect and Appreciation

Rebuilding a connection often involves acknowledging and appreciating the positive aspects of your past relationship. Recognize the qualities and actions of your ex-partner that you value, and express your respect for them.

Rebuilding Trust

Trust is a crucial component of any reconnection. Be honest and consistent in your words and actions, and give your ex-partner the time and space to rebuild trust in you. Trust is earned over time, and patience is key.

Collaboration and Compromise

Collaboration and compromise are vital when finding common ground. Be willing to work together, make concessions, and find solutions to the challenges that led to the divorce. This shows your commitment to rebuilding your relationship.

Professional Mediation

In some cases, professional mediation or therapy can be helpful in facilitating the reconnection process. A neutral third party can assist both you and your ex-partner in addressing issues and finding solutions.

Managing Expectations

It's important to manage your expectations during the reconnection process. Understand that the path to rebuilding a relationship is not always linear, and there may be setbacks along the way. Patience and resilience are essential.

Personal Growth and Independence

While reconnecting with your ex-partner is a significant goal, don't neglect your personal growth and independence. Continue to invest in yourself, your interests, and your well-being, as a healthy, self-sufficient individual can contribute positively to a rekindled relationship.

Nurturing the Connection

Reconnection is an ongoing process. Once you've re-established a connection with your ex-partner, invest in nurturing it. Spend quality time together, engage in shared activities, and continue to communicate openly and honestly.

Reconnecting with your ex-partner is a challenging but potentially rewarding endeavor. It's a step toward rekindling love, whether that love takes the form of a renewed romantic relationship, a friendship, or a co-parenting partnership. In the chapters to follow, we will explore how to further strengthen this rekindled connection and build a more loving future together. Remember, every step toward reconnection is a step toward healing and growth.

6

Chapter 6: Healing Wounds: Forgiveness and Letting Go

The wounds left by divorce can run deep, affecting not only your personal well-being but also your ability to rekindle love with your ex-partner. In this chapter, we delve into the profound process of forgiveness and letting go, which is essential for healing and moving forward after divorce.

The Power of Forgiveness

Forgiveness is a transformative and empowering process. It doesn't mean condoning or forgetting the pain caused by the divorce, but rather, it's a conscious choice to release the grip of anger, resentment, and bitterness. Forgiveness is a gift you give to yourself as much as to your ex-partner.

Self-Forgiveness

Before forgiving your ex-partner, it's crucial to forgive yourself. Recognize that you are human and made mistakes just like anyone else. Self-forgiveness is a fundamental step in healing and self-compassion.

Understanding the Why

Understanding the reasons behind your ex-partner's actions or decisions that led to the divorce can be a key part of the forgiveness process. It allows you to see the situation from their perspective, fostering empathy and compassion.

The Weight of Resentment

Resentment can be a heavy burden to carry. It can consume your thoughts and hold you back from moving forward. Letting go of resentment is an act of self-liberation and an important step toward rekindling love.

Release and Closure

Closure is not necessarily a conversation or a meeting with your ex-partner. It can be a symbolic act or a private ritual that represents your willingness to release the past. Closure is a powerful step in the process of letting go.

Rebuilding Trust

If you hope to rekindle love with your ex-partner, trust must be rebuilt. Forgiveness is the foundation for rebuilding trust. It's a signal that you are open to the possibility of healing and creating a future together.

Embracing a New Narrative

Reframe the story of your past relationship. Instead of viewing it solely through the lens of the divorce, consider it as a chapter in your life that brought valuable lessons and growth. This new narrative can help you release the grip of the past.

Practicing Mindfulness

Mindfulness techniques can help you stay grounded in the present and let go of rumination about the past. Techniques such as meditation and deep breathing can be useful in managing your emotions and reducing the impact of painful memories.

Seeking Professional Help

If you find forgiveness and letting go particularly challenging, consider seeking the assistance of a therapist or counselor. Professional guidance can provide you with tools and strategies to navigate this process effectively.

Healing and Growth

Healing and growth go hand in hand. By letting go of the past and forgiving, you open yourself up to personal growth and the possibility of a more positive and loving future, whether that's with your ex-partner or in new relationships.

Maintaining Boundaries

As you work on forgiveness and letting go, it's important to maintain healthy boundaries with your ex-partner. Forgiveness does not necessarily mean resuming the same dynamic as before. Boundaries help you protect your emotional well-being as you move forward.

Forgiveness and letting go are profound steps toward personal healing and the potential rekindling of love with your ex-partner. In the upcoming chapters, we will explore how these processes can contribute to building a more loving and harmonious future, both within yourself and in your relationships. Remember, forgiveness is a gift you give yourself, and letting go is a path to freedom and renewal.

7

Chapter 7: The Art of Effective Communication: Rebuilding Trust

Effective communication is the cornerstone of any successful relationship, and after a divorce, it becomes even more critical. In this chapter, we will explore the art of effective communication as a means to rebuild trust, enhance understanding, and rekindle love in your relationship with your ex-partner.

The Role of Communication

Communication is the bridge that connects people emotionally and intellectually. After a divorce, it becomes a vital tool for rebuilding the connection that may have been strained or broken. Effective communication is essential for rebuilding trust and creating a nurturing environment.

Active Listening

Active listening is a key component of effective communication. It involves fully concentrating on what your ex-partner is saying, without interrupting or formulating your response while they are speaking. It shows respect and empathy, fostering an open and honest exchange of ideas and emotions.

Empathetic Communication

Empathy is the ability to understand and share the feelings of another. It's a crucial aspect of effective communication, as it allows you to connect on a deeper emotional level. Expressing empathy by acknowledging your ex-partner's emotions can help rebuild trust and foster a more compassionate connection.

Non-Verbal Communication

Non-verbal cues, such as body language, facial expressions, and tone of voice, often convey more than words alone. Being mindful of your non-verbal communication is important, as it can impact the emotional tone of your conversations.

Clear and Direct Expression

Clarity in your communication is key. Avoid vague or ambiguous language, and express your thoughts, feelings, and needs clearly and directly. Ambiguity can lead to misunderstandings and unnecessary conflict.

Avoiding Blame and Criticism

It's important to avoid blaming and criticizing your ex-partner. Instead of using accusatory language, focus on "I" statements to express your feelings and needs. This approach reduces defensiveness and allows for more constructive discussions.

Conflict Resolution

Disagreements are a natural part of any relationship. Developing effective conflict resolution skills is essential for maintaining open and respectful communication. Work together with your ex-partner to find solutions to issues that arise.

Setting Healthy Communication Boundaries

Setting boundaries for communication is important, especially when emotions run high. It's okay to take a break from a conversation if it becomes too heated or unproductive. Respect each other's boundaries and return to the discussion when you're both calmer.

Building Trust Through Consistency

Consistency in your communication is essential for rebuilding trust. Keep your promises, be reliable, and show that you can be counted on. Trust is rebuilt over time through consistent actions.

Seeking Mediation or Therapy

In some cases, seeking professional mediation or therapy can be highly beneficial for improving communication and resolving lingering issues. A neutral third party can provide guidance and help you navigate challenging conversations.

Patience and Persistence

Rebuilding effective communication takes time and patience. It may not happen overnight, but persistence in improving your communication skills is key to creating a healthier and more loving connection.

Effective communication is a powerful tool for rebuilding trust and rekindling love in your relationship. In the chapters that follow, we will delve deeper into the intricacies of communication and explore strategies for strengthening your connection. Remember, communication is a continuous process, and by mastering it, you can create a more loving and harmonious future.

8

Chapter 8: Dating Again: Navigating New Relationships

After a divorce, many individuals embark on the journey of dating and exploring new relationships. In this chapter, we'll delve into the exciting yet sometimes challenging process of dating after divorce. By navigating new relationships with intention and care, you can continue on your path of personal growth and potentially find new love.

The Transition to Dating

Dating after a divorce is a significant transition. It's important to consider your readiness and motivation for dating. Make sure you're seeking new relationships for the right reasons, whether it's companionship, personal growth, or the pursuit of a loving partnership.

Self-Exploration and Discovery

Before entering the dating scene, take time for self-exploration and self-discovery. Reflect on the lessons and insights gained from your past relationship and divorce. Understand your values, needs, and deal-breakers in a new partner.

Setting Realistic Expectations

It's essential to set realistic expectations for dating. Understand that not every date will lead to a long-term relationship, and it's okay to experience some dating setbacks. Embrace the process of getting to know different people.

Communication and Honesty

Open and honest communication is crucial in the early stages of dating. Be upfront about your past and the fact that you are divorced. This transparency builds trust and helps potential partners understand your journey.

Building Confidence

Dating can be intimidating, especially after a divorce. Building your self-confidence is vital. Focus on self-care, self-compassion, and reminding yourself of your worth. Confidence is attractive and will make you more comfortable in the dating world.

Emotional Resilience

Being emotionally resilient in the face of dating challenges is important. Not every date will result in a connection, and rejection is a part of the process. Resilience helps you bounce back and maintain a positive outlook.

Balancing Dating and Parenting

If you are a parent, balancing dating and parenting responsibilities can be a unique challenge. It's crucial to find a balance that works for you and your children. Ensure that new partners respect your role as a parent.

Building Healthy Boundaries

Establish healthy boundaries in your new relationships. This includes setting personal boundaries for physical and emotional intimacy and communicating your needs and expectations clearly to potential partners.

Red Flags and Warning Signs

Be vigilant for red flags and warning signs in new relationships. If something feels off or uncomfortable, it's essential to trust your instincts and prioritize your well-being.

Learning from Each Relationship

Every dating experience provides an opportunity for personal growth and learning. Whether a date leads to a lasting relationship or not, each encounter can teach you something valuable about yourself and your preferences.

Patience and Timing

Timing is crucial in the dating world. Don't rush into new relationships; allow them to develop at a natural pace. Be patient with the process, and remember that the right person may come into your life when you least expect it.

Dating after divorce is a journey of self-discovery, personal growth, and the potential for new love. In the chapters that follow, we will explore the complexities of dating in more detail and provide strategies for navigating the challenges that may arise. Remember that each step you take in the dating world is an opportunity for growth and a chance to rekindle love in your life.

9

Chapter 9: Blending Families: Creating Harmony in a New Family Structure

For many individuals who remarry or enter into new relationships after divorce, blending families becomes a significant part of their journey. In this chapter, we'll explore the complexities and challenges of creating harmony in a new family structure. By navigating the path of blending families with care and intention, you can build a loving and supportive environment for all family members.

Understanding the Dynamics

Blending families involves merging two distinct family units into one. It's important to understand the dynamics and unique characteristics of both families to better anticipate challenges and opportunities.

Open and Honest Communication

Effective communication is critical in blended families. Encourage open and honest conversations among all family members. Create a safe space for everyone to express their feelings, concerns, and expectations.

Building New Relationships

Family members, especially children, may need time to adjust to the new relationships. It's important to be patient and allow these bonds to develop naturally. Foster positive interactions and create opportunities for shared experiences.

Defining Roles and Responsibilities

Clearly define roles and responsibilities within the new family structure. Discuss parenting roles, household duties, and financial responsibilities to ensure everyone is on the same page.

Navigating Conflicts

Conflicts are inevitable in any family, and they may become more complex in blended families. Develop conflict resolution strategies and teach family members how to handle disagreements with respect and understanding.

Encouraging Inclusivity

Create an inclusive family environment by including all family members in decision-making processes and activities. Avoid favoritism and make an effort to ensure that everyone feels valued and appreciated.

Honoring the Past

Recognize that family members may carry emotional baggage from their previous family structures. Acknowledge the importance of the past while focusing on building a positive future together.

Setting New Traditions

Establishing new family traditions and rituals can help solidify the bond within the blended family. Create meaningful activities that everyone can enjoy and look forward to.

Seeking Professional Guidance

In some cases, the challenges of blending families may necessitate the help of a family therapist or counselor. A neutral third party can provide guidance and facilitate productive discussions.

Individual Relationships

In addition to nurturing the family unit, maintain individual relationships with each family member. Spend one-on-one time with your partner, biological children, and stepchildren to strengthen your connections.

Patience and Flexibility

Blending families is a gradual process that requires patience and flexibility. Understand that it may take time for everyone to adjust and for the family dynamics to settle into a new, harmonious structure.

Fostering a Supportive Environment

Above all, create a supportive and loving environment in your blended family. Encourage kindness, empathy, and a sense of belonging among all family members.

Blending families is a complex but rewarding journey. In the chapters to come, we will explore specific strategies for addressing the challenges and celebrating the successes of creating harmony in your new family structure. Remember that each family is unique, and with patience, love, and intention, you can build a strong and loving blended family that contributes to the rekindling of love in your life.

10

Chapter 10: Strengthening Your Connection: Rekindling Love in a Blended Family

In a blended family, the goal is not only to create harmony but also to rekindle love and strengthen your connection with your partner and the entire family. In this chapter, we'll explore strategies for enhancing your connection and fostering love within your blended family.

Prioritizing Your Relationship

Amid the complexities of blended family life, it's essential to prioritize your romantic relationship. Dedicate time for one another, whether through date nights, weekend getaways, or simple moments of togetherness.

Shared Values and Goals

Discuss and establish shared values and goals within your blended family. Having a clear vision for your family's future helps align everyone's efforts and fosters unity.

Quality Family Time

Create opportunities for quality family time. Participate in activities that the entire family can enjoy, from game nights to family outings. These shared experiences strengthen bonds and create positive memories.

Strengthening the Parenting Partnership

As co-parents, strengthen your partnership by maintaining a united front. Agree on consistent parenting strategies and discipline methods to ensure a cohesive approach to raising your children.

Acknowledging Individuality

Respect and celebrate the individuality of each family member. Encourage your stepchildren to pursue their interests and hobbies, and create an environment where everyone's uniqueness is valued.

Embracing Flexibility

Flexibility is key in blended families. Be open to adjusting schedules, roles, and routines as needed to accommodate everyone's needs and adapt to changing circumstances.

Encouraging Communication

Keep the lines of communication open with your partner and the entire family. Encourage children to express their feelings and concerns, and ensure they know their voices are heard and respected.

Navigating the Blended Family Hierarchy

Blended families often involve complex hierarchies. It's important to discuss and establish clear roles and expectations within the family structure, ensuring that all family members feel secure and valued.

Family Meetings

Hold regular family meetings to discuss important matters and address concerns. These meetings provide a forum for constructive conversations and collaborative problem-solving.

Celebrating Achievements

Celebrate each family member's achievements, big or small. Recognition and encouragement create a positive and loving atmosphere in your blended family.

Seeking Professional Support

In cases where challenges persist, consider seeking the assistance of a family therapist or counselor. A professional can provide guidance and strategies for addressing specific issues.

Embracing Patience and Resilience

Rekindling love in a blended family is an ongoing journey that requires patience and resilience. Recognize that there may be ups and downs, but the effort is worth it for the love and connection you're building.

Promoting a Loving Environment

Above all, work together to promote a loving and supportive environment within your blended family. Love, kindness, and understanding are the pillars that will help you create a harmonious and fulfilling life together.

Strengthening your connection and rekindling love in a blended family is a rewarding and ongoing process. In the chapters that follow, we will delve deeper into the unique dynamics of blended families and provide strategies for addressing the challenges while nurturing the love that binds you together. Remember, every effort you invest in your blended family contributes to a brighter and more loving future for all.

11

Chapter 11: Overcoming Challenges: Navigating the Complexities of a Rekindled Relationship

Rekindling love in a relationship after divorce is a profound journey, but it's not without its challenges. In this chapter, we'll explore the complexities of rekindled relationships and provide strategies for overcoming obstacles and building a stronger and more loving connection with your partner.

Acknowledging the Past

Acknowledge the past, including the reasons for the divorce and the pain it may have caused. Discuss these experiences with your partner in a respectful and open manner. Addressing the past can help both of you gain closure and move forward.

Managing Expectations

Rekindling a relationship does not mean that all previous issues have disappeared. Be realistic about the challenges you may face. Understand that healing and rebuilding trust will take time.

Rebuilding Trust

Trust, once broken, takes time and consistent effort to rebuild. Be trustworthy and demonstrate your commitment to your partner through your words and actions. Offer trust and allow it to be earned in return.

Effective Communication

Continue to prioritize effective communication in your rekindled relationship. Open, honest, and empathetic conversations are the foundation for understanding each other's needs and resolving conflicts.

Seeking Professional Help

In some cases, seeking couples' therapy or counseling can be beneficial in navigating the complexities of a rekindled relationship. A therapist can provide guidance and facilitate productive discussions.

Respecting Individual Growth

Recognize that both you and your partner have likely grown and changed since the divorce. Respect each other's personal growth and understand that evolving as individuals can enrich the relationship.

Balancing Independence

While rekindling love is a shared journey, it's important to maintain your independence. Pursue your interests, spend time with friends and family, and continue to invest in your personal growth.

Patience and Resilience

Rekindling love is a process that requires patience and resilience. Be prepared for setbacks, and understand that they are part of the journey. Continue to work together to overcome challenges.

Navigating Parenting

If you have children, parenting can add another layer of complexity to your rekindled relationship. Be united as co-parents and communicate effectively about your children's needs and well-being.

Creating New Memories

While acknowledging the past is important, focus on creating new memories together. Enjoy shared experiences and adventures that strengthen the connection you're rebuilding.

Celebrating Your Love

Take moments to celebrate your love and commitment to each other. Whether through special occasions, surprise gestures, or simply expressing your love, celebrating your relationship is essential.

Embracing the Journey

Above all, embrace the journey of rekindling love. Recognize that it's a unique and transformative experience, and despite the challenges, it holds the potential for a more profound and enduring connection with your partner.

Rekindling love in a relationship after divorce is a significant undertaking, and it can be filled with complexities. In the chapters that follow, we will explore how to navigate these challenges with grace and build a love that stands the test of time. Remember, the journey itself is a testament to your love and commitment.

12

Chapter 12: A Lasting Love: Sustaining and Nurturing Your Rekindled Relationship

Rekindling love is a transformative journey, but it doesn't end with the initial spark. In this final chapter, we'll explore the keys to sustaining and nurturing your rekindled relationship, ensuring that the love you've rebuilt continues to flourish.

Commitment and Dedication

Maintain a deep commitment to your rekindled relationship. Dedicate yourself to the journey of love, understanding that it requires ongoing effort and care.

Quality Time Together

Continue to prioritize quality time with your partner. Regularly spend time together, whether through date nights, weekend getaways, or simple moments of connection. These shared experiences strengthen your bond.

Communication and Understanding

Effective communication remains essential in sustaining love. Keep the lines of communication open, practice empathy, and understand that your partner's needs and feelings may evolve.

Respecting Individual Growth

As both you and your partner continue to grow as individuals, respect each other's personal journeys. Embrace the uniqueness of your partner and support their ongoing personal development.

Rekindle the Romance

Keep the romance alive in your relationship. Surprise each other with gestures of love and affection. Find new ways to express your passion for one another.

Handling Challenges Together

Challenges are a part of every relationship. Approach challenges as opportunities for growth, and work together to overcome them. Resilience and teamwork strengthen your love.

Embracing Change

Be open to change and adaptation in your relationship. Understand that the dynamics and needs of your partnership may shift over time, and flexibility is essential.

Seeking Professional Support

If your relationship faces significant challenges, consider seeking the assistance of a couples' therapist or counselor. Professional guidance can help you navigate complex issues and improve your relationship.

Maintaining Personal Growth

Continue to invest in your personal growth and well-being. A healthy, self-assured individual contributes positively to a loving and lasting relationship.

Celebrating Milestones

Celebrate the milestones of your relationship. Whether it's an anniversary, a significant achievement, or a moment of personal growth, recognize and celebrate these moments together.

Honoring Your Love Story

Acknowledge and honor your unique love story. Reflect on the journey you've traveled together, and use it as a source of inspiration and appreciation for your partner.

Never Stop Learning

A lasting love is one that continues to evolve. Never stop learning about each other, about love, and about what makes your relationship special.

Rekindle the Flame

Finally, never forget the journey that brought you to this point. Rekindle the flame of love with regular reminders of the special moments and milestones in your relationship.

A lasting love is a treasure, and it's a testament to your commitment and care for each other. In your rekindled relationship, the journey is ongoing, and the potential for enduring love is limitless. Remember, with continued dedication and nurturing, your love can continue to grow and flourish, enriching your lives for years to come.

www.ingramcontent.com/pod-product-compliance
Lightning Source LLC
LaVergne TN
LVHW041246200726
843507LV00013B/2840